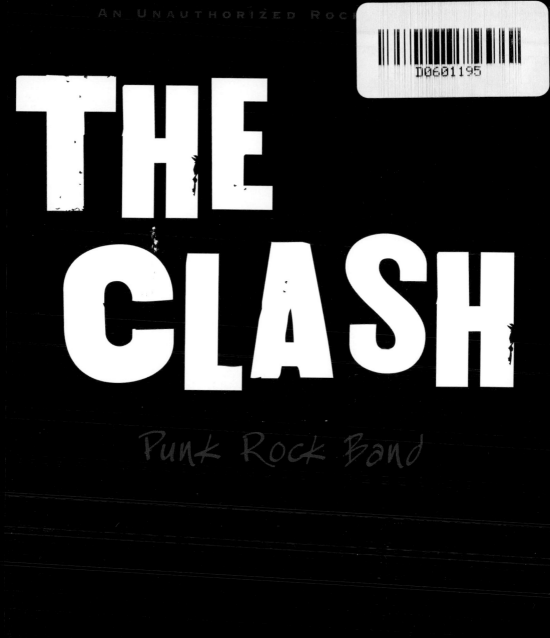

THE CLASH

Punk Rock Band

Other Titles in

Library Ed. ISBN-13:
978-0-7660-3031-2
Paperback ISBN-13:
978-0-7660-3623-9

Library Ed. ISBN-13:
978-0-7660-3236-1
Paperback ISBN-13:
978-1-59845-210-5

Library Ed. ISBN-13:
978-0-7660-3379-5
Paperback ISBN-13:
978-1-59845-212-9

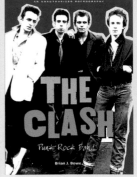

Library Ed. ISBN-13:
978-0-7660-3232-3
Paperback ISBN-13:
978-1-59845-211-2

Library Ed. ISBN-13:
978-0-7660-3234-7
Paperback ISBN-13:
978-1-59845-208-2

Library Ed. ISBN-13:
978-0-7660-3028-2
Paperback ISBN-13:
978-0-7660-3620-8

Library Ed. ISBN-13:
978-0-7660-3029-9
Paperback ISBN-13:
978-0-7660-3621-5

Library Ed. ISBN-13:
978-0-7660-3027-5
Paperback ISBN-13:
978-0-7660-3619-2

Library Ed. ISBN-13:
978-0-7660-3026-8
Paperback ISBN-13:
978-0-7660-3618-5

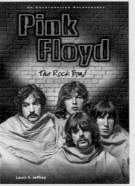

Library Ed. ISBN-13:
978-0-7660-3030-5
Paperback ISBN-13:
978-0-7660-3622-2

Library Ed. ISBN-13:
978-0-7660-3233-0
Paperback ISBN-13:
978-1-59845-213-6

Library Ed. ISBN-13:
978-0-7660-3231-6
Paperback ISBN-13:
978-1-59845-209-9

THE CLASH

Punk Rock Band

Brian J. Bowe

REBELS OF ROCK

Enslow Publishers, Inc.
40 Industrial Road
Box 398
Berkeley Heights, NJ 07922
USA
http://www.enslow.com

To Heather, my punk rock heroine

Library of Congress Cataloging-in-Publication Data

Bowe, Brian J.
  The Clash : punk rock band / Brian J. Bowe.
    p. cm. — (Rebels of rock)
  Includes bibliographical references and index.
  Summary: "A biography of British punk rock band the Clash"—Provided by publisher.
  ISBN 978-0-7660-3232-3
  1. Clash (Musical group)—Juvenile literature. 2. Rock groups—England—Juvenile literature.
3. Punk rock musicians—England—Juvenile literature. I. Title.
  ML3930.C5235B69 2010
  782.42166092'2—dc22
  [B]   2009006470

ISBN-13: 978-1-59845-211-2 (paperback ed.)

Printed in the United States of America

052010 Lake Book Manufacturing, Inc., Melrose Park, IL

10 9 8 7 6 5 4 3 2 1

Illustration Credits: Associated Press, pp. 64, 77, 87; © CBW/Alamy, p. 55; Ian Dickson/Rex USA/Courtesy Everett Collection, pp. 16, 23; Getty Images, p. 25; Fraser Gray/Rex USA/Courtesy Everett Collection, p. 20; © Bob Gruen/www.bobgruen.com, p. 67; © Homer Sykes Archive/Alamy, p. 48; ITV/Rex USA/Courtesy Everett Collection, p. 83; LFI London, p. 30; © Network Photographers/Alamy, p. 8; Photofest, p. 79; Ray Stevenson/Rex USA/Courtesy Everett Collection, pp. 6, 35, 38, 42–43, 50.

Cover Illustration: Redferns/Getty.

CONTENTS

The Clash in 1976

1

A RIOT OF MY OWN

It was a hot summer day in London in 1976, and thousands of revelers were gathered in the Notting Hill section of the city to have a good time. It was the annual Notting Hill Carnival, which was a celebration of Caribbean culture staged by London's growing immigrant population.

But there was tension in the air that day. There was a history of racial violence in that section of London, with riots in 1958 and 1964. Much of the problem was poor relations between the black community and the police.

On that August day in 1976, on Portobello Road, police tried to arrest a pickpocket and were met by angry bystanders. The streets exploded; people began throwing bricks, smashing windows, and setting things on fire. More than 160 people had to be taken to the hospital, and 66 people were arrested. Police sealed off roads and closed pubs and a subway station. Selwyn Baptiste, one of the organizers, was disappointed. "This was supposed to be about fun and love—not violence," he said.[1]

PEOPLE ENJOYING THE NOTTING HILL CARNIVAL IN 1976.

In the crowd that day were members of the Clash: Joe Strummer, Mick Jones, and Paul Simonon, along with their manager, Bernard Rhodes. And they weren't merely spectators.

"We were there at the very first throw of the first brick," Strummer said. "This was one time where people went 'We've had enough and we're going to say so now.'"[2]

But Strummer was aware that, while he was a part of the riot, it wasn't really *his* riot.

"We participated in the riot, but I was aware all the time that it was a black people's riot, i.e. [that is] they had more of an ax to grind and they had the guts to do something physical about it," Strummer said.[3]

Inspired, Strummer wrote a song called "White Riot," in which Strummer sang about his desire to start a riot of his own.

"The song was about white people getting up and doing it for themselves," said Clash bassist Simonon, "'cause our black neighbors were doing it for themselves insofar as the riots and whatever, so it's time for the white people to get on with their own situation, which I suppose was the beginning of the punk thing."[4]

And for the next nine years, the Clash set out to create something that was entirely their own, that captured the explosive energy of a riot through punk rock. A line from

"White Riot" could be considered a punk-rock mission statement—"Are you taking over? Or are you taking orders?"

That riot was an electrifying moment for the new band. Not only did it give them the inspiration for the song "White Riot" but it helped solidify the group's antiracist political beliefs and sense of justice for all.

"Punk rock, at the heart of it, should be protest music," said Strummer. "Punk rock for me was a social movement. . . . We tried to do the things politically we thought were important to our generation and hopefully would inspire another generation to go even further."[5]

From that moment in 1976 until the band's demise in the mid-1980s, they were intent on taking over. And, in many ways, they succeeded.

The Clash was the first punk-rock band to leap from underground acclaim to massive mainstream success. But they professed a do-it-yourself philosophy that encouraged fans to make music themselves, and they always tried to bridge the gap between the band and the audience. They questioned authority, but along with their anger was a playful sense of the beauty of diverse cultures and styles of music.

They also stretched the boundaries of what could be considered punk. They added elements of rockabilly, rhythm and blues, reggae, hip-hop, and jazz to their songs.

"It was really the Clash who, having begun as a defining punk band, then attempted to see what else they could turn their hands to, applied their talents to a whole other bunch of styles and influences, and demonstrated that while you still have the punk gene, as long as you don't lose it, you can take it anywhere," said rock journalist Charles Shaar Murray.[6]

With that combination of brutal honesty and musical experimentation, the Clash were a massive influence on other bands.

U2 singer Bono said, "The Clash was the greatest rock band. They wrote the rule book for U2."[7]

"They combined revolutionary sounds with revolutionary ideas," said Rage Against the Machine's Tom Morello, "and their music launched thousands of bands and touched millions of fans."[8]

The Clash's influence has endured long after the band broke up. "The Clash are the British punk band who made the most inroads into America," said Gerard Way from My Chemical Romance. "They're the most important British punk band to Americans—no question."[9]

WHO ARE THE CLASH?

The main members of the Clash were singer and rhythm guitarist Joe Strummer, singer and lead guitarist Mick Jones, bassist Paul Simonon, and drummers Topper Headon and Terry Chimes, who were in the band at different times.

Joe Strummer

Joe Strummer was born John Graham Mellor in 1952. Strummer's father was born in India. He came to London and joined the Foreign Office, which was responsible for the British government's relationships with other nations. Strummer was born in the Turkish city of Ankara, and as a child, his family spent time in Cairo,

Egypt; Mexico City, Mexico; and Bonn, Germany. That international upbringing accounted for some of the Clash's expansive worldview. Through his early life, Strummer adopted several different personas.

When he was nine years old, Mellor's parents sent him to boarding school, and he would only see them once a year, when he would visit them. Mellor would visit his parents in such countries as Iran, Rhodesia (now Zimbabwe), and Malawi. He would return from those trips with stories and exotic records.

Mellor felt rejected by his parents when they sent him to boarding school.

"It's easier, isn't it? I mean, it gets the kids out of the way, doesn't it?" Strummer said sarcastically to writer Caroline Coon in 1976. "It was great! You have to stand up for yourself. You get beaten up the first day you get there."[1]

Those childhood difficulties helped him develop an independent personality that was always questioning authority. "Authority is supposedly grounded in wisdom, but I could see from a very early age that it was only a system of control and it didn't have any inherent wisdom," he said.[2]

At boarding school, he learned another tough lesson—in that environment, you either were a bully or you got bullied. "I quickly realized that you either became a power or you were crushed," he said.[3]

While he was at boarding school, he discovered rock and roll. The first rock song that blew him away was "Not Fade

Away" by the Rolling Stones. "We were stuck up in school, and there was no way of getting out to get it, but I do remember the radio delivering it," he said. "The song moved like a steam train, and that was the moment I went rock and roll forever, the moment I said, 'Yeah . . . wow!'"[4]

At that time, even though he was inspired by rock and roll, he had no musical abilities.

"I wasn't in any choir, I didn't learn any instrument, nothing. But we were fervent listeners," he said. "It seemed to be a mystical world where only mythical beings could actually play."[5]

In 1970, Mellor's older brother, David, committed suicide, which was a traumatic event in his life. The two were very different—David was shy and quiet while his brother was outgoing. Before David died, he had gotten very interested in Nazism and had joined a racist political party in England called the National Front.

"I was deeply affected by it, and I don't know if I've come to terms with it yet, because it's a mysterious thing to try and understand," Mellor said of his brother's death.[6]

After high school—and shortly after his brother's death—Mellor went to art school at Central School of Art and Design, where he adopted the name "Woody," inspired by folksinger Woody Guthrie.

Woody Guthrie was a folksinger from the United States who wrote songs like "This Land Is Your Land." Explaining the name change years later, Mellor said he decided to name himself after Woody Guthrie because of "the humanity of his music. That stuff was inspiring—it was a 'one day hopefully I'll be as good as him' nickname. But I don't think everyone who called me Woody had even heard of Woody Guthrie, they just thought it was a groovy name."[7]

When he was at art college, Mellor found himself getting restless.

"From school I went straight into art college, and after a year I just went off and did absolutely nothing," he said. "For at least two years I was just bumming around. Everyone's gotta bum around. I worked on a farm but stayed 'round London most of the time, and when I was 21 I thought right, I'll get really serious now and I'll learn to play the guitar."[8]

In 1972, Mellor bought a ukulele and began to play on the London subway—known as the Tube—with Tymon Dogg, who played violin. Playing music in public for donations from passersby is called "busking." Mellor learned some Chuck Berry songs but didn't play them. Instead, he collected donations for Dogg—until one fateful day.

"The train emptied at one end of the corridor. One second the corridor was empty, the next it was packed with people steaming through. It was like, now or never, playing to this full house. That was the first time I remember performing on my own," he said.[9]

In 1975, Mellor adopted yet another persona, adopting

Mick Jones (left) and Joe Strummer on stage in 1977

the stage name Joe Strummer. His new nickname poked fun at his guitar style, which featured intense rhythmic strumming and little in the way of fancy ornamentation. "I called myself Joe Strummer because I can only play all six strings at once, or none at all," he said. [10]

Later in his life, Strummer discussed the difference between John Mellor and Joe Strummer. Being Joe Strummer, he said, "allows you to do stupid things like write ditties on the back of [cigarette] packets. If you were rational it would be a stupid thing to do. But it's about being irrational. I never stop thinking about life, asking, 'Why did I do that?' Kind of blundering through life is my method." [11]

Mick Jones

Michael Geoffrey Jones was born in 1955 in London. His father, Thomas, was a taxi driver. His mother, Renee, sold jewelry and was a big fan of Elvis Presley. His maternal grandmother, Stella, also lived with the family.

When he was eight years old, his parents divorced, and Jones went to live with his grandmother. That event had a big impact on Jones's life.

"Psychologically it really did me in," said Jones in 1976 of his parents' split. "I wish I knew then what I know now. Now I know it isn't that big of a deal. But then, at school, I'd be there with this word 'divorce, divorce' in my head all the time. But there was no social stigma attached to it because all the other kids seemed to be going through the same thing. Very few of the kids I knew were living a sheltered family life."[12]

To deal with the split, Jones turned to music. "Maybe music became an escape for me. I think it did to a certain extent," Jones said. The first records he bought with his own money were Jimi Hendrix's *Smash Hits* and Cream's *Disraeli Gears*.[13]

Another escape for Jones was professional soccer—which is popular in England, where it is called "football." He collected autographs of all of the football stars of the time. "I knew all the hotels where they stayed, and I'd wait outside and ask them to sign my *Topical Times Football Book*," he said. "Some of them were really kind . . . and some of them were particularly mean. The way I was treated then has always stuck in my mind." Jones added that he thought of those experiences later in his life, when it was *his* turn to sign autographs.[14]

His mother moved to the United States, and she helped fuel Mick's passion for rock music. "She used to send me *Rock Scene* and *CREEM*, with those great photos by Bob Gruen," Jones said. "That was my total inspiration. I was lucky she was living in America. When I saw that stuff, it was like, wow! There weren't many people over here who were into that sort of [underground U.S.] music in those days. Only a handful."[15]

Many of his school friends were starting bands, and eventually Mick started playing guitar, too.

"I was the last kid on my block to pick up a guitar, 'cause all the others were repressing me and saying, 'No, you don't want to do that, you're too ugly, too spotty, you stink!' and I believed 'em. I was probably very gullible. And then I realized that they weren't doing too well," Jones said. "I said . . . 'I can do that!'"[16]

In 1973, Jones and his grandmother moved to Wilmcote House, a gray concrete twenty-story high-rise building overlooking a stretch of highway known as the Westway. "It was really a kind of horrible place to live," Jones said. "At the time I was living there I didn't think much about it, but I'm shocked when I go back there, because people are still living in it. It's worse than it was. It gets worse every year."[17]

Even after he was in the Clash, Jones continued to live occasionally with his grandmother. "I always came back to my Nan, because I loved her," Jones said.[18]

Paul Simonon

Paul Gustave Simonon was born in 1955 in the Brixton section of London, but his family moved a lot.

Simonon's parents divorced when he was ten years old. First he moved with his mother and stepfather to Italy.

"It was all a bit bohemian, wandering around these beautiful streets by day, and being taught by my mum for a few hours in the evening," he said. The word *bohemian* is used to

Paul Simonon in 1980

describe an artistic lifestyle that doesn't conform to that of conventional society.[19]

Simonon returned to London to live with his father, who was a painter and ran a much more disciplined household. Simonon's father made him do his homework and paint every day. "I learned the technical stuff from a mate of my dad's who knew how to do glazes and underpainting," Simonon said. "It was invaluable, really. He'd hand me a brush and go, 'Here, Paul, I have to go to work, finish off that fox for me.'"[20]

Because of his background, Simonon developed an independent streak and was a bit of a loner.

"I suppose my upbringing made me resilient in some way," Simonon said. "What I remember most, though, is that feeling of always being the new boy at school. That was kind of tough. I have absolutely no friends from school, no connections from back then. I was always moving on. I gained a certain independence from that experience."[21]

Like many British rock stars, Simonon went to art school. But unlike some of the others, he really desired to be an artist. In fact, it was Simonon's traditional style of painting that led him to leave art school, where the teachers all seemed to favor modern American art.

Simonon said his creative side was always a part of his personality. "As a kid, I always wanted toy soldiers to play with, so I used to paint them on pieces of paper. Create them for myself," he said. "In a way, it's still the same. Whether I'm in a good mood or a bad mood, painting takes me out of myself. And I've realized lately that it often resolves things for me."[22]

Not only did Paul's talents influence the Clash's visual presentation, but he was a massive fan of Jamaican reggae music, which had a big impact on the band's music.

"The sounds I remember hearing was probably reggae, really," he remembered. "I used to pass by a lot of houses where there was West Indian music playing."[23]

Topper Headon

Nicholas Bowen Headon was born in 1955 in Kent, England. His parents were both musicians who played the piano and sang. His family moved to Dover, where his father was a school headmaster—which helped develop Headon's mischievous side. "When your father's the headmaster, to be accepted you had to be a lot more naughty than the other kids," Headon said. "I got into trouble to show that I wasn't the teacher's pet."[24]

His two passions were music and soccer. When he was fourteen, though, he broke his leg playing soccer and was confined to bed for several weeks. His father bought him a drum set to help him exercise his leg. Headon taught himself piano and began playing drums at school. His favorite drummers were jazz players Buddy Rich and Billy Cobham.

Once he started playing drums, he would practice all the

Topper Headon in the late 1970s

time. "Drumming became my first addiction. I'd play for eight hours a day," he said.[25]

Drumming may have been his first addiction, but, unfortunately, it wasn't his last. Headon discovered drugs at a young age and would struggle with a devastating drug addiction throughout his life. He started smoking marijuana at seventeen, and he began experimenting with other substances like amphetamines and barbiturates.

Strummer said Headon's drug use eventually destroyed Headon's ability to play with the Clash. "[Playing drums] is like nailing a nail into the floor. It's a precise thing. The beats have to be there and when Topper got addicted, he couldn't play anymore. It doesn't work with drums," Strummer said.[26]

Becoming addicted to drugs was one of the big regrets of Headon's life. "If I could do it all again, or not do it all again, the only thing I would change is that I wouldn't take cocaine or heroin," Headon said. "Until I took cocaine and heroin my life was brilliant, but since then it's been hard work."[27]

Once he joined the Clash, Headon became widely known by his stage name, Topper—a name given to him by Paul Simonon. "Coming up with nicknames was my department and decided to call him Topper because of his ears," Simonon said. "He looked like a character from a comic book called *Topper.*"[28]

Terry
Chimes in
1982

Terry Chimes

Terry Chimes was the first drummer for the Clash, and he rejoined the band after Headon was fired.

Chimes was born in 1956 in London. He was the middle child between two brothers, both of whom were also musicians. His younger brother played bass, while his older brother was a classical music percussionist.

"He's three years older than me, and when he was eighteen, he was going to the Royal College of Music," Chimes said. "And so I thought, 'If you're going to do that, I'm going to be a rock and roll star!'"[29]

Chimes was also fascinated by science, and he was torn between being a musician and studying medicine.

After he left the Clash for the second time in 1982, Chimes left the music business entirely and became a chiropractor. "I felt it was time to completely change—and over the time I'd been a musician, I'd already become a non-drinking, non-smoking, non-drug-taking vegetarian who does yoga," Chimes said.[30]

NO ELVIS, BEATLES, OR THE ROLLING STONES

The 1960s were known as a colorful era of peace and love, both in the United States and in England. British artists like the Beatles, the Rolling Stones, and Cream were making music that sounded like colorful swirls that promised a brighter tomorrow. "All you need is love," sang the Beatles in a song reflective of those times.

But a decade later, that brighter tomorrow hadn't arrived. For the youth in England in the mid-1970s, the promise of the hippie generation had crumbled into dust. Things looked bleak. England's economy was in crisis and unemployment was higher than it had been in decades. The use of hard drugs like heroin was on the rise.

Along with the economic and social problems, there was a growing level of class discontent among the poor working class in England. "England is a highly static society, with a strongly defined ruling class and a narrow definition of the acceptable. If you fall outside it for any reason, you're marginal," wrote author Jon Savage, adding that pop music "is a place where many of them meet, as dreamers and misfits from all classes, to transform, if not *the* world, then their world."[1]

A new generation of rock fans was growing up disappointed that the promise of the hippie dream was broken. They were looking to create a new culture—one where they belonged. For many of them, that new culture was punk.

"Suddenly you didn't have to be alone," Savage wrote of the new punk movement. "You *submerged*. You had a good time by having a bad time. You were full of the poison. . . . You attacked the generation of World War Two: all that they could not express you'd flaunt in their faces, stiff upper lip morphing into blank stare and violent gesture," wrote Savage. "[T]his was tough stuff, telling England what it did not want to hear."[2]

Caroline Coon, a journalist who briefly managed the Clash, described that era as a time of "strange silence, like after an explosion, when everything blown into the air is falling to earth. The Swinging Sixties party was over. People were reeling in shock. Some were regrouping. Some were watching, wondering what would survive once the debris had settled."[3]

Part of the problem, Coon wrote, was with the rock stars of the time. "The spirit of Britain seemed punishing and mean," she wrote. "White musicians who had created the hippie soundtrack—those still alive—had traded rebellion for Establishment. Mega-rich, chummy-with-royalty rock stars were disdainfully out of touch with teenagers. Few resented their making millions, but what they did with the profits mattered. Where was any sense of hippie altruism and community? It was as if white rock 'n' roll had changed sides."[4]

Joe Strummer remembered the pre-punk period as a dull time, filled with poverty. One way to get around the poverty was "squatting," which refers to the practice of taking over an abandoned building and living in it. There was a large squatting scene in London in the mid-1970s.

"In 1974 there didn't seem to be any color in life," Strummer said. "There were rows and rows of buildings, all abandoned, boarded up by the council [local government] and left to rot. For what reason I don't know. There were hordes of people in London who couldn't afford to pay rent—not the rents that were being asked. So the only thing to do was to kick in these abandoned buildings and then live in them. Thank god that happened because if it hadn't happened I would never have been able to get a group together, because we were in a situation where we were absolutely penniless."[5]

Strummer moved into a squat on 101 Wallerton Road with some other musicians. They started a band named after their squat's address—the 101ers. The band, which had a revolving lineup, played a style of music known at the time as pub rock.

Writer Allan Jones remembered an early 101ers show: "The 101ers in many ways are crude, loud, untutored, technically deficient, and their set seems to consist of nothing but covers of classic rock and roll and old R&B chestnuts—the staple repertoire of what was known as pub rock. But in other ways that matter more—energy and passion among them—they are unforgettable, a glorious, raucous noise at a time when most rock music is bloated, pompous, overplayed."[6]

The band rented a room upstairs in a pub and charged admission. "That's how we learned to play, by doing it for ourselves, which is kind of like a punk ethos," Strummer said. "You've got to be able to go out there and do it for yourself, because nobody's going to give it to you."[7]

In May 1975, the101ers began playing regular shows at a club called the Elgin, which lasted until the following January. "The place used to be packed," Strummer said. "What I remember is glasses smashing and fights breaking out and dogs running around."[8]

In the meantime, Jones was trying to start a band called the London SS. These days, Jones is embarrassed by the band's name, which has Nazi overtones.

"Somehow I believe a sort of karma stopped that group

Punk emerged in the 1970s. Joe Strummer and others started a band called the 101ers in the early 1970s.

being a success because it would have been a very negative thing to be propagating," Jones said.[9]

The band played songs by the Rolling Stones, along with little-known groups like the Flaming Groovies and the MC5. They were also inspired by a groundbreaking double album of American garage rock called *Nuggets*. This collection of unknown and unpolished rock music was compiled by music journalist and guitarist Lenny Kaye. When that compilation was released in 1972, "it instantly became an essential part of everyone's collection in the '70s, just at the time when rock was at its lowest ebb (in terms of popular participation, at least) and many people were itching for an excuse to shake things up," wrote Greg Shaw, an influential rock writer and founder of the punk rock-record label Bomp.[10]

The band had a revolving door of members. Many future punk-rock and new-wave stars played with London SS, including Tony James from Generation X; Brian James and Rat Scabies from the Damned; Chrissie Hynde from the Pretenders; and future Clash members Paul Simonon, Terry Chimes, and Topper Headon.

Around this time, Jones met Bernard Rhodes, who would become the Clash's manager and would have a large influence on the group. Born in Russia, he moved to London in the 1950s. By the 1960s, he was a part of the London rock scene, spending time with the Who, the Rolling Stones, and Marc

Bolan of T.Rex. He was also interested in the radical politics of the time.

In the early 1970s, Rhodes began designing T-shirts and went into business with Malcolm McLaren, who would go on to manage a band called the Sex Pistols.

Jones was wearing one of Rhodes's designs when the two met in 1976 at the Nashville Rooms club. "I was always on the lookout for other musicians, because in 1976, there weren't that many people who were into what I was into," Jones said. "I asked Bernie Rhodes if he was a piano player and he said 'No, I'm not, but I make those tee shirts.'"[11]

The two formed a bond quickly. "I wanted a partner, so until I met Joe, Bernie was my partner. We hit it off straight away. We knew we were going to do it, Bernie seemed to know more than me about what we were going to do," Jones said. "Sometimes in the early days I lost heart, but he always saw a way through."[12]

Jones was still trying to find the right combination of musicians for his new band. Simonon remembered his audition.

"I came in on the London SS when it was on its last legs. Mick had seen this mate of mine, who was a drummer, in the street and told him they were rehearsing and to come down, so I went with him," remembered Simonon. "They were rehearsing drummers and looking for a singer, so Mick asked me if I was a singer. I said no, I've just turned up with me mate. I had a go at Jonathan Richman's 'Roadrunner,' but I'd never heard the song before in my life."[13]

Jones decided Simonon had potential and started trying to teach him how to play. "I didn't want to be the bass player, I wanted to be the guitarist. They had all the flash stuff going," Simonon said. "But I remember Mick trying to show me an E [chord] shape on a guitar. After about an hour, I was still getting nowhere, so Mick got me a bass instead."[14]

Jones and Simonon teamed up with a guitarist named Keith Levene. "He was a young bloke, and he was a guitarist," said Jones. "I think Bernie probably encouraged me to get something together with him."[15]

There was a lot of action brewing on the London music scene. A band called the Sex Pistols had just begun, and many consider them to be the first British punk-rock band. They—along with the Clash and many other bands—would set off a punk-rock explosion two years later.

Founded in 1975 in the same scene that spawned the Clash, the band was fronted by the sneering singer Johnny Rotten, backed up by the thick, muscular guitar of Steve Jones and the rhythm section of drummer Paul Cook and bassist Glenn Matlock (who was later replaced by Sid Vicious). The band took aim at the government, the British royal family, and the upper class with songs like "Anarchy in the U.K." and "God Save the Queen."

"In England, the group was considered dangerous to the

THE SEX PISTOLS AND OTHER BANDS EXPLODED INTO
THE LONDON PUNK ROCK SCENE.

very fabric of society and were banned across the country; in America, they didn't have the same impact, but countless bands in both countries were inspired by the sheer sonic force of their music, while countless others were inspired by their independent, do-it-yourself ethics," wrote Stephen Thomas Erlewine in the *All Music Guide*.[16]

The punk scene was growing, and the Sex Pistols were leading the way.

Filmmaker Don Letts—who directed many of the Clash's music videos—echoed that sentiment. "That was the thing about punk. It made you want to be involved, not a spectator. But the stage was full up, so I picked up a super-8 camera and started filming the bands. I'd never had any training," he said.[17]

Jones was in the audience one fateful night, when the Sex Pistols opened for Strummer's 101ers. "I remember the Pistols show was curtailed suddenly by a fistfight that actually spread from the stage," said Jones. "We all saw this and it kind of overshadowed Joe's performance afterwards. It was like the old and the new, sitting in the same place. I know that it was a marking point for Joe."[18]

For Strummer, watching the Sex Pistols had an immediate impact. He was inspired to shed the old music he was playing and become a part of the new punk world.

Jones, Simonon, Levene, and Rhodes thought Strummer would be the perfect frontman for their new band. Rhodes and Levene approached Strummer at London's 100 Club.

"I went outside to talk to Bernie, we were hanging out by the bus stop and Bernie gave me an ultimatum and he said 'Look, I'll give you 24 hours. I've got to go on this thing, so you're in or you're out,'" Strummer said. "So I thought about it all night and I thought about it all day and I rang him and he picked up and I just said I'm in, and that was before meeting Mick or Paul."[19]

Strummer went to his first rehearsal with the new band at a squat on Davis Road. Right from the beginning, he helped set the Clash's political tone, changing a song Jones wrote about a girl called "I'm So Bored with You" into a political statement called "I'm So Bored with the U.S.A."

"We were always talking about how there was too many McDonald's here," Jones said. "Although we'd been brought up on American TV shows and all that, there was still too much of an American influence. That was really what the song was about."[20]

The band brought in drummer Chimes. "They had something different about them," Chimes said. "I didn't particularly like them, but there was something about the way they did things that was saying, 'We mean business. We are going to get there. Nothing's going to stop us.'"[21]

The new band tried out several different names—including the Weak Heart Drops, the Outsiders, the Psycho Negatives, and the Mirrors—before Simonon came up with the band's name, after noticing how often the word *clash* was used in newspaper headlines.

"Well, it's a clash against things that are going on," Simonon explained, "the music scene, and all that we're hoping to change quite a lot."[22]

As punk rock was beginning in London, a similar movement had been growing in New York. The flagship New York punk band, the Ramones, came to London in July 1976 for a pair of shows. The band's self-titled debut album had just been released. The performances were the two-year-old band's first shows outside the United States. The Ramones played short,

THE CLASH ON STAGE IN LONDON IN 1976

catchy, and simple songs with volatile energy, creating a wall of sound unlike anything the audiences had heard before. Members of the Clash, the Sex Pistols, and other future legends of British music were in the audience. Those shows were inspiring for those aspiring punk rockers.

"It can't be stressed how great the first Ramones album was to the scene," Strummer said, "because it gave anyone who couldn't play the idea that it was simple enough to be able to play. We all used to practice along with it. Paul and I spent hours, days, weeks playing along to the record. Anyone could see where the notes went and it gave everyone confidence. It was the first word of punk, a fantastic record."[23]

The Ramones also inspired Jones. "When we first heard the Ramones album, how influential that was, because it was just like totally really short songs, really hard attack, no non-sense, and it was just like cut down, bare to the bone, you know and it was like, that was inspiring," said Jones.[24]

The Ramones' back-to-basics approach energized the Clash, while the bleakness of life in England inspired a series of volatile, anger-filled songs that dealt with the issues of everyday life. Rhodes had a big influence on the band's lyrical content.

Just two months after the Ramones came to London, *Sounds* writer Chas de Whalley reviewed a Clash performance at the Roundhouse.

"Joe Strummer's Clash—the best new band of the year? Well, some would claim as much," de Whalley wrote. "At least you can guarantee that any band formed by the 101ers guitar-ist will bristle with fire and energy. Unfortunately at the Roundhouse the Clash had little more on offer . . . the warmth and love of the old pub rocking 101ers has been traded for a new aggression and belligerence."[25]

That show was Levene's last with the band. "Keith left the band because he couldn't be bothered to come to rehears-als," Jones said. "And then I think Joe said, 'Well, don't bloody come at all, then!'"[26]

That December, the Clash went on the road in support of the Sex Pistols on a tour called the "Anarchy Tour." Just before the tour began, the Sex Pistols had spoken obscenities on national television. In the controversy that followed, fourteen of the scheduled twenty-one concerts were canceled.

The controversy also made punk rock a household word in England "It really put punk on the map. Every truck driver and builder and your grandmother and your uncle knew what punk rock was now about," Strummer said.[27]

The Clash's first songs were fiery assaults on society. "London's Burning" expressed youthful frustration with its chorus of "London's burning with boredom now." In the song "1977," the chorus included the declaration: "No Elvis, Beatles or the Rolling Stones"—a signal that there was a new direction in music.

Only a year after forming, the Clash signed a record deal with CBS records, and many accused the band of selling out. But, for the band, it meant a bit of regular income.

"I've been turning it over in my mind, but now I've come to terms with it. I've realized that all it boils down to is perhaps two years of security," Strummer said. "We might have an argument with CBS and get thrown off! For me it has been a gift from heaven. Before, all I could think about was my stomach. A lot of the time me and Paul did nothing else but wonder where our next meals was coming from. We were hungry all the time."[28]

And Strummer's prediction came true—the Clash would feud with CBS Records for the rest of their career.

The Clash's self-titled debut was recorded in February 1977. The band's musical skills were still raw and unpolished, but what they lacked in ability they made up for in energy.

"There was a lot of struggling with our instruments at the start," Jones said. "It was that struggling, learning to play—it made it alive, it made it real, it made it something that wasn't like anything else."[29]

In the British magazine *Sounds,* reviewer Peter Silverton was thrilled with the album. "At its most basic level The Clash is the best white dance album of the seventies," he wrote. "And when it comes to raw rock 'n' roll energy, it makes almost anything you ever heard sound decidedly limp and polite." He added "If you don't like the Clash, you don't like rock 'n' roll. It really is as simple as that. Period."[30]

Rolling Stone's Charley Walters wrote: "The Clash is something different. Better than any other punk rock album, *The Clash* convincingly vents its outrage and frustration . . . *and* backs them with simple, careful, driving rock. The Clash knows that volume doesn't always mean power and that melody and subtlety don't necessarily weaken their stance."[31]

Citing crude sound quality, the album wasn't released in the United States but sold one hundred thousand copies as an import. An American version of the album was released in 1979 featuring several different songs.

The Clash were becoming known for powerful live performances. One of the things that made touring hard on the Clash was a common practice of the time of audience members spitting on bands to show appreciation—a practice called "gobbing."

Johnny Green, a member of the Clash's road crew, remembered: "You couldn't play a gig in the punk years that was not just covered in gob. From the moment you stepped behind the amplifiers to front the stage, you were covered in gob, and it didn't matter who you were, but especially good if you could gob on the Clash."[32]

The practice of gobbing began after an exchange of spit between Sex Pistol Steve Jones and future drummer for the Damned named Rat Scabies. While it was a common way for fans to express appreciation for the bands at early British punk-rock shows, Jones called the practice "disgusting," and by 1978, the Clash asked audiences not to spit. That year, Strummer had to spend two weeks in the hospital after he became ill with the liver ailment

In the mid-1970s, The Clash became known for their powerful concerts.

hepatitis B. Strummer blamed the sickness on gobbing after he accidentally swallowed the spit of an audience member.

The band was starting to take off, but drummer Chimes quit because he didn't share the Clash's political stance. "It took on a life of its own. It was like joining a cult," Chimes said. "I wanted to enjoy playing music—and they wanted to suffer. It was serious from the moment you got up in the morning, until the moment you went to sleep."[33]

The Clash auditioned 205 drummers before hiring Headon, whose powerful, precise, and hard-hitting style perfectly complemented the Clash's punk-rock sound, and whose versatility would help move the band's style forward.

"There's a rule in rock 'n' roll that says 'You're only as good as your drummer,'" Strummer said, noting that Headon could also play funk, soul, and reggae music. "Finding someone who not only had the chops but the strength and stamina to do it was just the breakthrough for us."[34]

LONDON CALLING

The punk-rock explosion of 1977 was a signal that England was changing. The members of the Clash were open about their appreciation of other styles of music from around the world—particularly Jamaican reggae and rhythm and blues. But there were elements in British society that weren't as open-minded.

During World War II, many nationalities from throughout the British Commonwealth (a collection of colonies from around the world) fought for Great Britain. In 1948, the government passed the British Nationality Act, which made citizens of any of the colonies also citizens of Great Britain. By the mid-1950s, immigrants were becoming more common. Thanks to immigration from former British colonies in India, Pakistan, and the Caribbean, England was becoming increasingly multicultural.

Some white people blamed those immigrants for the high unemployment in the country, and others were afraid increasing immigration posed a threat to British culture. Those fears led to the founding of the National Front, a political party founded in the mid-1960s with the aim of ridding Britain of its multiracial immigrants.

National Front spokesman James Merrick said people found comfort in the face of unemployment and other social ills from his party. "Sometimes people call us up and talk for hours. There is no other place for them to turn. They're just bursting with frustration," Merrick said.[1]

The National Front appealed to many of the same disaffected youths who were attracted to punk rock. In response to the National Front, a group called the Anti-Nazi League was formed. In April 1978, some eighty thousand people gathered in London's Victoria Park for a concert put on by an organization called Rock Against Racism (RAR), in conjunction with the Anti-Nazi League. The Clash was one of the bands on the bill that day.

Poly Styrene, singer for the punk band X-Ray Spex, was also one of the performers. "I think it has achieved a lot," she said. "I think racism isn't so blatant as it was in the '70s, when it was socially acceptable to call people all kinds of names because of their different backgrounds. I can't speak for other artists, but for me, RAR was something that made me think about other people's lives and struggles."[2]

The concert solidified the Clash's reputation as an antiracist band. "The Clash's powerful performance was a triumph," wrote Chris Salewicz.[3]

Some electrifying footage of Rock Against Racism is included in a feature film called *Rude Boy,* which is a part-documentary, part-dramatic film about the punk-rock scene of the late '70s. The film tells the story of Ray Gange, who plays a member of the Clash's road crew. In addition to the Rock Against Racism footage, there is a wealth of other volatile performances of the band shot in 1978 and early 1979. The Clash band members also act in the film.

After seeing the final product, the band distanced itself from the film and tried to stop it from being released. Mick Jones said manager Bernard Rhodes arranged the band's participation in the movie, and the group was having problems with him. "It seemed like Bernie set up the film *Rude Boy,* and then halfway through he stopped working with us, and we were just making it up as we went along. And they were filming it," Jones said.[4]

In 1980, Rhodes said the band's fight with him is what soured them on the movie. "It was hard work to get the group interested in the project because they were losing interest in me," Rhodes said. "In the end they were going to get paid a

In 1978, Rock Against Racism (RAR) put on a concert in London,

certain amount, but basically it was supposed to be a labor of love."[5]

When the film was finally released in 1980, critical reaction was lukewarm. "Like many films which use novice actors it hovers uncomfortably between fiction and documentary in its narrative sections and it still seems flabby in parts despite the editing marathon it took to reduce it to its present dimensions. But the simple fact is it's a must for Clash-lovers," wrote Phil Sutcliffe in *Sounds*.[6]

When the Clash went into the studio to record its second album, the band's eyes were on America, where the first album still hadn't been released. To produce 1978's *Give 'Em Enough Rope*, the Clash turned to Sandy Pearlman, who had produced a series of successful records with American heavy metal band Blue Öyster Cult.

Pearlman's production style was precise and polished, which was often at odds with the Clash's impulsiveness.

The group was continuing to feud with manager Rhodes, which added tension to the studio, and Pearlman convinced Strummer and Jones to come to the United States to mix the album.

"I told them that if they didn't get out of England they would really have trouble finishing the record because of their constant fights with Bernard," Pearlman said. "It was down to where all sorts of silly stuff would happen. They would come in nine hours late because they'd gone to Paris to play and

The Clash performed during the RAR concert in 1978.

missed a plane or something. Or Bernard would come in and they'd argue for five hours and then no one would be able to play. They were literally unable to work. It was deemed a normal thing for them to have business meetings during recording sessions."[7]

The album received conflicting reviews when it was released. *Trouser Press* reviewer Ira Robbins applauded the album's production, writing that "[w]hat Pearlman has done is, as the title says, allow them enough studio freedom through expertise to make an album the way they see fit."[8]

On the other hand, *Rolling Stone* reviewer Greil Marcus knocked the album's production, writing that *Give 'Em Enough Rope*'s sound "seems suppressed: the highs aren't there, and the presence of the band is thinner than it ought to be. The record doesn't *jump*."[9]

But while the band's success was growing, not everything was going well for the Clash. The band fired Rhodes, and the day after a press reception for *Give 'Em Enough Rope*, Strummer and Topper Headon were selling clothes at an open-air market. "We're broke, man, so you just have to do what you can," Strummer said. "Bernie's kicked us out of our rehearsal studio and changed the locks."[10]

After firing Rhodes, the band asked friend and writer Caroline Coon to manage them on a trial basis.

The Clash toured America for the first time in 1979. Like the response to *Give 'Em Enough Rope,* the reviews of the tour were varied. Some critics were elated by the Clash's energy, while others thought it was just a bunch of noise.

Reviewing a show for *NY Rocker*, Howie Klein wrote: "No one could accuse the Clash of being just another rock and roll band. The intensity alone—without even getting into the sheer quality of the performance—alternates between invigorating and stupefying. Little Richard was great; so were the Stones—but there's nothing like the Clash."[11]

Writing in the *LA Weekly*, Don Snowden had a similar opinion. "From the opening riff of 'I'm So Bored With The USA' to the closing chords of 'White Riot,' the Clash set was an onslaught of pure energy by a band that resembles a rock and roll attack squad," Snowden wrote. "Lead guitarist Mick Jones leaped and sprinted from one end of the stage to the other while bassist Paul Simonon coolly loped around front stage. And I've never seen a performer so completely wrapped up in his music physically as Strummer—slashing away at his battered Telecaster, mouth agape, left leg pumping like piston and eyes often wide open with the look of a man who's seen his worst nightmares come to life ten feet in front of his face."[12]

But the *Washington Post* was critical of the band's performance at the Ontario Theater in Washington, D.C. "The Clash are latest sensations in the world of punk, that riotously ridiculous form of music that refuses to die. Like all self-respecting musicians of their sort, their music was a droning mass of power chords, static rhythms and off-key ranting that was propelled by sheer energy and not much else," wrote Harry Sumrall. "Stumbling across the stage, dressed in tight black pants and greased-back hair, they were like visions from an earlier age of rock and roll. What their set lacked in musicality, it more than made up for with excitement, but after awhile even too much excitement becomes a bore."[13]

When the Clash began recording its next album, the band had a new political force to fight against. In 1979, the band recorded *London Calling*, which is considered by many to be one of the greatest albums of all time. That same year, Margaret Thatcher was elected Prime Minister of Great Britain. Thatcher was a member of the conservative Tory party with a political style that earned her the nickname the "Iron Lady."

The Clash were working hard to move beyond the blistering aggression of its early punk songs. "There was a point where punk was going narrower and narrower, painting themselves into a corner. We thought we could just do any kind of music," Jones said.[14]

Because the band's previous rehearsal space belonged to Rhodes, the Clash found a new space behind a car repair garage called Vanilla. "We needed that bit of seclusion and privacy," Jones said. "I think at that time we needed to regain our composure."[15]

They spent an intense period of writing and rehearsing at

Vanilla. The band's only recreation was playing soccer. "We'd play football 'til we dropped and then start playing music," Strummer said. "It was a good limbering-up thing."[16]

There was a new member of the Clash entourage around this time—a man named Kosmo Vinyl who served as the band's press liaison. He said the time at Vanilla was beneficial for the band.

With a new batch of material, the Clash entered the studio to begin recording the new album, which had a greater musical depth than before.

"We always tried to play just as good as we could. What we play now is what we can do," Strummer explained. "It wouldn't be fair to do ranting music, because we've mastered a time-change. We can play in another rhythm. So there's just no point. We do a bit of ranting, just to keep it up, but we don't do it all the time. We do something now which we couldn't do before."[17]

To record *London Calling,* the Clash worked with producer Guy Stevens, who was a known eccentric. A DVD released with the twenty-fifth anniversary version of *London Calling* shows the producer jumping around, throwing chairs, swinging ladders, and trying to increase the excitement level in the studio.

While he raised the excitement level in the studio, he also made the band members comfortable. "Guy Stevens was really great, he made me feel really at ease," Simonon said.

"If I played wrong notes, he didn't care."[18]

The sessions yielded an abundance of material— enough for a double album—and the Clash fought with CBS Records, insisting that the label release the double album and sell it at a single-album price. "I'd say it was our first real victory over CBS," Strummer said.[19]

IN 1979, THE CLASH RELEASED *LONDON CALLING.*

London Calling was released in December 1979. Its iconic cover features a picture of Simonon smashing his bass onstage. It featured two of the band's most recognizable songs, the title track and Jones's "Train in Vain." It also featured "Brand New Cadillac," "Lost in the Supermarket," and "Guns of Brixton," which was written and sung by Simonon.

The Clash made their first music video for the song "London Calling," which was directed by Don Letts—who was partially responsible for exposing punk rockers to reggae music. In the early days of punk, Letts was a DJ at a club called the Roxy, and he ran a clothing store called Acme Attractions, and he played reggae in both places. He is of Jamaican descent, and is a Rastafarian—a religion closely linked to reggae music. Reggae superstar Bob Marley was the most famous Rasta and he was influential in Letts's development both spiritually and politically.

The Rastafarian faith developed in Jamaica and is centered around the belief that Ethiopian king Haile Selassie was god—who they call Jah—returned to earth. Rastas are known for a hairstyle known as dreadlocks, in which long hair resembles ropes.

London Calling was released to great critical acclaim. John Rockwell called *London Calling* "symbolically the first important rock album of the 1980s."[20]

"This is an album that captures all the Clash's primal energy, combines it with a brilliant production job by Guy Stevens and reveals depths of invention and creativity barely suggested by the band's previous work," Rockwell wrote.[21]

Rolling Stone critic Tom Carson's review also admired the album's power: "Merry and tough, passionate and large-spirited, *London Calling* celebrates the romance of rock and roll rebellion in grand, epic terms. It doesn't merely reaffirm the Clash's own commitment to rock-as-revolution. Instead, the record ranges across the whole of rock and roll's past for its sound, and digs deeply into rock legend, history, politics and myth for its images and themes. Everything has been brought together into a single, vast, stirring story—one that, as the Clash tell it, seems not only theirs but ours."[22]

In *Rolling Stone*'s 1980 critics' poll, critics named the

Clash the band of the year and *London Calling* the album of the year. But even though the album was critically acclaimed, the Clash didn't top the charts. *London Calling* peaked at number 9 in the United Kingdom and number 27 in the States.[23] Punk—which had also inspired another new style of music called "new wave"—didn't have mass appeal yet.

Because of the outlandish behavior and shocking fashions of some of the punk bands, particularly the Sex Pistols, some saw the label "new wave" as a way to make the new style of music more acceptable to the masses. Eventually, new wave evolved into a distinct form of music. Some of the major new wave bands included Devo, Duran Duran, the Police, the Pretenders and Talking Heads. While the Clash were definitely a punk band, because they branched out into many other genres of music, they also can be considered a new-wave band.

Around that time, Pink Floyd's *The Wall* album was at the top of the charts, along with Led Zeppelin's *In Through the Out Door*, The Eagles' *The Long Run,* and Fleetwood Mac's *Tusk*. With all of the critical applause, why wasn't punk or new wave more popular?

"The answer is simple: the American rock audience, in general, prefers music that's safe anchored in a solid pop tradition, as the success of the new wave's tamer examples (Blondie, the Knack, Talking Heads) can truly testify," wrote Robert A. Hull in the *Washington Post*. "As with rockabilly and American punk, the hostile and aggressively experimental factions of the new wave (British punk rock, in particular) have proven too threatening."[24]

The Clash followed the critical acclaim of *London Calling* with a bold move. The triple-LP *Sandinista!* was the product of a burst of creativity that saw the band expanding its sound even further into reggae, soul, and R&B. The sprawling album was recorded in Manchester, England; New York; and Kingston, Jamaica, between February and December 1980.

The band went to Kingston for a session with reggae producer Mikey Dread, and ended up in a dangerous situation.

The Rolling Stones had just been in Kingston recording, and they had given money to all of the local gangsters, who expected the Clash to do the same. But the Clash didn't have money, so they had to make a quick exit and didn't record anymore.

The Clash went to New York to continue recording in Electric Lady studios, without any new songs written. They recorded the bulk of the next album over the next three weeks, writing songs as they went along.

"Everything was done in first takes, and worked out twenty minutes beforehand. What we did was go to the core of what we are about—creating—and did it on the fly and had three weeks of unadulterated joy," Strummer said.[25]

The original plan was not to release a triple album. "*Sandinista!* was originally going to be a double album,"

Simonon said. "But what happened is we decided we wanted to bring out a single a month, and the first one we put forward was 'Bankrobber,' and I think the head of the record company said they didn't like it. They said it sounded like David Bowie backwards."[26]

With the single-a-month plan scrapped, the Clash decided to release a triple album, but CBS records wasn't thrilled with that idea either—especially with the Clash insisting that it be priced as a single album. CBS eventually agreed to release it, but on the condition that it only counted as one album against the band's commitment to the label, and that the band give up performance royalties on the first two hundred thousand copies of the album.

The album was named after the Sandinista revolutionary group in Nicaragua that had come to power after a revolution in 1979.

Once again, critical reaction to the album was a mixed bag. *Rolling Stone* gave the album its top five-star rating. Reviewer John Piccarella said *Sandinista!* was too long, but that the album contained many high points.

"If the ambition of *London Calling* was to recast the whole of (largely American) rock and roll history, then *Sandinista!* wants a place in the cultural traditions of the world," Piccarella wrote. "While the Clash are still saying that they can do anything and anything they do is worth hearing—

it's less as if they're trying to top themselves than that they're overexcited about passing on everything they've learned."[27]

But other reviewers were not as kind. Many condemned the album's length and uneven quality.

Van Gosse, writing in the *Village Voice,* wrote that "there's material here for an incredible gempacked single, or an excellent double, but a triple set is ridiculous, even if it is cheap."[28]

Talking about the album years later, Strummer conceded that *Sandinista!* wasn't perfect, but he said he was still pleased with it.

"I can only say I'm proud of it, warts and all, as they say. It's a magnificent thing, and I wouldn't change it even if I could. And that's after some soul searching," Strummer said. "Just from the fact it was all thrown down in one go. It's outrageous, and then released like that—it's doubly outrageous, it's triply outrageous."[29]

If Strummer's goal was to make people aware of the Sandinista movement, he was successful.

"I never knew who the Sandinistas were or where Nicaragua was," said U2 singer Bono. "The lyrics of Joe Strummer were like an atlas. They opened up the world to me, and to other people who came from kind of a blank suburbia."[30]

5

SHOULD I STAY OR SHOULD I GO?

In February 1981, the Clash rehired Bernard Rhodes as its manager at Joe Strummer's insistence and against Mick Jones's wishes.

Rhodes, when he came back, compared the Clash to a classic car, saying that "it was a rusty wreck and I had to do it up and put my updated engine back in there."[1]

England itself was in rough shape in 1981—there was trouble all over the country. There was a law called the "Sus Law," where police could stop anybody if they were even suspected of planning a crime. That law hit black youths particularly hard, and it sparked three days of rioting in Brixton in April.

"The streets were just full of bricks, mortar, stones, smashed bottles, a carpet," said one of the protesters, Alex Wheatle, on the twenty-fifth anniversary of the riots. "Black kids were being purged off the streets, they were being beaten up in cells. The establishment had to acknowledge that. I stood up and I fought with them."[2]

In July 1981, the Toxteth section of Liverpool erupted in nine days of rioting. Tension in inner-city Liverpool had been rising because of unemployment, racism, bad housing, and poor education. Police officers were accused of beating blacks and planting drugs on them to arrest them. That anger spilled out all over the city, with rioters throwing gasoline bombs and paving stones. Police shot back with tear gas. In the end, up to one thousand people were injured and seventy buildings demolished.

While the riots were going on, the Clash was in New York—a fact that led many to criticize the band for rejecting its political roots, forged in the Notting Hill Carnival riots five years earlier.

The Clash was in New York to play seven shows at a Times Square club called Bonds International Casino. The fire department discovered that too many tickets to the shows had been sold, so they canceled a performance.

Strummer said, "There had been such a heavy demand for tickets that the club box office had oversold the nights. The Fire Department were tipped off and closed the whole thing down. . . . We decided to play out however many tickets had been sold for those gigs and we ended up doing 15 shows in a row, including a Saturday matinee for people under the age of the licensing laws."[3]

Even though the band was in the middle of its own controversy, they were thinking about the riots in England. "We were sitting there in New York saying, 'it's ridiculous us being here and this going on,'" said Rhodes. "But I don't know whether the riots were that major in terms of people being clear about what was going on."[4]

Rhodes continued: "The Clash are interested in politics rather than revolution. Revolution sets a country back a hundred years. Revolution is very, very dangerous. I don't think we ever were revolutionary. I think we were always interested in the politics of the situation. And I think we still are. But I think England is less interested."[5]

As the Clash grew more successful, some in the music press began to question the band's commitment to its early political stances. Strummer criticized the press in an article in the *NME*, saying, "If they're teaching the readers to hate us, then I'd like to ask the *NME* who they're teaching the readers to trust? Which groups? Which ideas? I'm looking hard, and I can't see anybody."[6]

The Bonds shows earned the Clash a lot of attention. "We were presented with a situation that escalated beyond control. We were on the news," Strummer said. "It was great, checking

IN 1981, THE CLASH HELD A NEWS CONFERENCE IN NEW YORK TO DISCUSS THEIR BONDS CONCERTS.

into New York and you're on the evening news. That was fantastic."[7]

However, the pace of the shows was draining for the band.

Photographer and friend of the band Bob Gruen played bugle before the encore each night at Bonds, and he said the run of shows was an important moment in Clash history.

"Bonds was a big thing because it seems that the bigger a group gets the more distant they get from their audience," he said. "But the bigger the Clash got the more they wanted to do for their audience to give back. . . . At Bonds, when it really got out of hand and the promoter had oversold the shows, instead of refunding half the money they said, 'Well, if we sold twice the number of tickets, we'll just play twice the number of shows.' What band does that for the same money?"[8]

It was an electric time in New York, as hip-hop music was just beginning to gain popularity. Strummer remembered the influential hip-hop radio station WBLS providing the sound-track for that summer.

Soon, the Clash were part of that soundtrack, when WBLS began heavily playing an instrumental version of the Clash's rap song "The Magnificent Seven," adding dialogue from movies.

The Clash were really the first band to bridge the gap between punk rock and rap.

"Bond's was great because of the chaotic, insane energy of the whole thing," said Def Jam records cofounder Rick Rubin, who has produced artists from the Beastie Boys to Slayer to Johnny Cash. "They were the first band to really embrace that cross-cultural revolution. They brought reggae to rock fans. In America everyone loves reggae because of the Clash. It was the same with hip-hop—I don't think the Beastie Boys would have been as into hip-hop if it wasn't for the Clash. The Beasties were really influenced by those Bond's shows," Rubin said.[9]

Boston Globe reviewer Steve Morse gave an electrifying

account of one of the Bonds shows. "To say [the Clash] were magnificent is an understatement. They performed like men possessed, churning out two hours of music that rocked the mind with its working-class," he wrote.[10]

If *Sandinista!* had multiple personalities, when the Clash went into the studio in mid-1981 to begin recording the follow-up, the group's leaders were torn on which of those personalities would win out. "Strummer wanted a single LP, full of good old fashioned rock and roll," wrote Keith Topping in *The Complete Clash*. "Jones wanted another sprawling-experimental *Sandinista!*-style collection of ambient textures and radical new sounds."[11]

Mick Jones told *Rolling Stone* that his goal was to have a hit record. "We'd like to be the successes that Van Halen are," said Jones. "We want to make people listen."[12]

Jones's wish would soon come true—people would listen. Despite the tensions in the band, the Clash were recording what would become their most commercially successful album. But the growing problem between band members would lead to the band's disintegration.

The Clash recorded the album, *Combat Rock,* in New York between April 1981 and January 1982. The tension between Jones and Strummer was so bad that the two worked on their overdubs at separate times, making sure they weren't in the studio at the same time. Jones did the first mix of the album,

Joe Strummer in New York City in 1981

coming up with a fifteen-song double album that the rest of the band didn't like.

First the four band members tried to remix the record themselves during a run of shows in Australia. "We were working around the clock," Strummer said. "I had a set of engineers to mix with, then I'd collapse and Mick would come in with fresh engineers, and I'd have a sleep on the floor."[13]

Finally, the band hired producer Glyn Johns to remix the album. Johns had previously worked with the Rolling Stones, the Who, the Beatles, and the Faces.

Combat Rock was finally released in May, 1982. Topper Headon called the style "a more international type of music" that featured "the funk influences, the reggae influences, the jazz influences . . . put into our own form for the first time."[14]

When Strummer spoke to *Rolling Stone*'s Peter Hall, he was fired up. "The trouble with this interview," Strummer said, "is that you're interviewing me as though I'm a success, and I feel I'm a failure. I only see the disappointments. We're angry because everything we do turns to ash. We're not fulfilled yet. But there will be a time when our work is done."[15]

Jones was likewise filled with frustration. "We'd like to have people's ears. We want to make them listen! We're not content. We want more, and I do and don't think we'll get it, but I suspect we'll have a good go at it."[16]

Strummer was fighting against a growing sense of materialism and consumerism.

"I want to tell people that they're being conned, that we're all being conned and we're lapping it up," Strummer said. "Working people are born without anything—no house, no toys, nothing. Obviously, they want to get a hold of something, and when they think they've got theirs, they don't want to let it go. But neither the haves nor the have-nots are happy. The working class are trying to get where the upper-middle class are, and the upper-middle class are more scared than any people I've ever seen. If you sit back and look at everything, it's a big joke."[17]

When *Combat Rock* was released, it seemed particularly relevant to what was going on in the world at the time. Great Britain went to war with Argentina over the Falkland Islands in the South Atlantic. The islands were home to a population of British people, and Britain attacked after Argentina's right-wing military dictator General Galtieri ordered an invasion of the islands. The British prime minister, Margaret Thatcher, ordered the military to try to take the islands back. Eventually, though, the British prevailed and recaptured the Falkland capital of Port Stanley.

Combat Rock received largely positive reviews in the music press. *Rolling Stone* reviewer David Fricke gave it four out of five stars, writing: "This record is a declaration of real-life emergency, a provocative, demanding document of classic punk anger, reflective questioning and nerve-wracking frustration."[18]

"Above all else, *Combat Rock* is an album of fight songs," Fricke added. "*Combat Rock* may not have the answers, but it may be our last warning: sign up or shut up."[19]

NME reviewer Charles Shaar Murry called it "a very *clear* album: the work of people who know exactly what they want to say and exactly how they want to sound."[20]

The Clash's critical acceptance and popularity was growing far beyond the punk-rock faithful. In the jazz magazine *Down Beat,* Michael Goldberg wrote: "If you listen to one rock and roll band in the next year, make it the Clash. You will discover music and lyrics as rich as anything Bob Dylan or the Rolling Stones created in the '60s, back when rock and roll mattered, back when rock was more than the uptempo elevator music one mostly hears by bands like Journey on the radio today."[21]

Combat Rock featured the Clash's two biggest hits— "Rock the Casbah" and "Should I Stay or Should I Go?"

"Rock the Casbah" was written by Topper Headon, who also played most of the instruments. "One day I went into the studio on my own because I don't actually know what notes I'm playing, so rather than try to tell everyone what to play I went and recorded piano, and then the drums and then the bass," Headon said. "I was thinking that it would just, you know, show them the way it could go but they all said 'great, let's keep it.' Mick put guitar on it, Joe put the vocals on and it was done."[22]

Strummer wrote the song's lyrics, taking a band in-joke and transforming it into a commentary on turmoil in the Middle East.

"We found that whenever we played a tune on the *Combat Rock* sessions, it would be six minutes minimum. After a few days of this, Bernie came down to the studio . . . and he said, 'Does everything have to be as long as a raga?'"[23] A *raga* is a type of music from India in which musicians improvise over a melody, often for long periods of time.

Strummer continued: "From then on we called everything we did ragas. . . . I got back to the Iroquois Hotel that night and wrote on the typewriter 'The King told the boogie men you got to let that raga drop.'"[24]

After he wrote that first line of the song, Strummer then began thinking about the situation in Iran—where he had lived for a time as a child. In 1979, an Iranian Muslim cleric and teacher named Ayatollah Ruhollah Khomeni returned to the capital of Tehran from exile in Paris. Khomeni led a revolution that overthrew the repressive shah (king) of Iran. Revolutionary committees "effected drastic changes throughout the country," wrote historian Arthur Goldschmidt, Jr. "Royal symbols were destroyed, in actions that ranged from blowing up monuments to cutting the shah's picture out of the paper money. Poor people seized and occupied the abandoned palaces. Streets were renamed, textbooks rewritten, political prisons emptied (soon they would be re-filled), and agents of the old regime tried and executed."[25] A group of revolutionaries seized the United States embassy in Tehran and held 63 American hostages for 444 days.

Khomeni's government proved to be very anti-Western, and that development inspired Strummer's lyrics for "Rock the Casbah."

The video for "Rock the Casbah" featured a man in traditional Arab clothing and a man dressed as an Orthodox Jew dancing and driving in a Cadillac car through oil fields in Texas, with an armadillo running around. Once again, Don Letts directed the video.

"The Clash were like four sticks of dynamite," said Letts. "On the cue of 'ACTION' these guys just went off. The armadillo was the mascot of Texas and was added for a bit of humor. Most people there had never seen a live one; only dead as ashtrays or handbags. For the scenes with the armadillo I had to crawl on my hands and knees backwards blowing at it to get it to walk towards the camera."[26]

On the other hand, "Should I Stay or Should I Go?" avoided deep political messages in favor of pure punk rock. Jones wrote the song as a return to the Clash's roots. "It was just a good rockin' song, our attempt at writing a classic," Jones said. "When we were just playing, that was the kind of thing we used to like to play."[27]

Just before *Combat Rock* was released, a series of events happened that would change the course of Clash history. First, on the eve of a British tour in April, Strummer disappeared for three weeks, causing the tour to be canceled. *Rolling Stone* reported that "[w]hile some cried hoax, the London police aided in a search for Joe, who was last seen on his way to Paris with his girlfriend Gabby."[28]

In fact, Strummer *was* in Paris. "I only intended to stay for a few days, but the more days I stayed, the harder it was to come back because of the more agro [aggravation] I was causing that I'd have to face there."[29]

Rhodes orchestrated the stunt, but the manager didn't expect Strummer to actually disappear. The singer said that he needed a break.

Two days after Strummer returned to London, the Clash announced that Headon had been fired, with original drummer Terry Chimes rejoining the band only five days before an American tour began.

Initially, the split was reported as Headon growing tired of the band's politics. "I think the Clash is the greatest," Headon said in *Rolling Stone*. "But the band is more than just music. I agree with their political stance, but I didn't enjoy living it twenty-four hours a day."[30]

But soon, the band began talking about the real reason Headon was fired: his heroin addiction.

"What he was up to sort of made a mockery of what the

group was about, and what Joe was writing about," Simonon said.[31]

Years later, in the Clash documentary *Westway to the World,* Headon expressed sorrow over letting the band down. "Looking back on it, you know, I was out of control," he said.[32]

"I felt a lot of guilt about that, because if I'd kept my act together, I could see the band possibly still being together today in a way," Headon added. "I'd like to kind of apologize to them for kind of letting the side down, for going off the rails. But I think if it happened again, I'd probably do the same thing. I'm just that sort of person, you know?"[33]

With Chimes on the drum stool, the band hit the road. In a great irony, it is Chimes playing the drums in the video for Headon's "Rock the Casbah," which received frequent airplay on MTV and helped launch the song into the Top Five on the music charts.

The Clash opened for the Who on a U.S. tour in the fall of 1982. They played New York's Shea Stadium, where Letts filmed videos for "Should I Stay or Should I Go?" and "Career Opportunities."

Strummer had a difficult time adjusting to the Clash's increasing success. "Standing there singing the songs while it got bigger and bigger towards the end, for some reason I started to feel worse and worse. It's something to do with what those songs are saying," Strummer said. "They were all right when we were part of the audience, part of a movement. Once it became a thousand miles removed from that, I began to freak out."[34]

A recording of that show was released in 2008 as a live album called *Live at Shea Stadium*. Jones reflected on the show, saying: "To me, I like to hear the four individuals of the band and how they jell together. It's kind of magic. I like to hear it as an overall thing. And, the way this has been put together, you can hear everything clearly, the amalgam [combination] of four people and how it all clicks together."[35]

In May 1983, the Clash played the US Festival, put on by Apple Computer cofounder Steve Wozniak. The Clash picked a public fight with Wozniak, demanding that he donate one hundred thousand dollars to a children's summer camp or they wouldn't play.

When they finally took the stage two hours late, the band stood in front of a banner that said "THE CLASH NOT FOR SALE." Van Halen lead singer David Lee Roth, who was also playing the festival, famously mocked the Clash for taking life too seriously.

The success of *Combat Rock* was confusing for the band—particularly for Strummer. "It caused him a huge confusion because, on one hand, he wants to be, you know, hugely successful. He wants to be, I think like many, you know, artists of the kind that get up on stage," said Chris Salewicz. "He wanted to feel validated as a human being. He wants to feel his voice was literally heard. But it's very confusing being the man of the people and then suddenly having, you know, a ton of money in your bank account."[36]

Chimes said that Strummer was starting to chafe at the band's success. "He didn't let himself be happy," Chimes said. "The problem with Joe was that he'd feel guilty if he was comfortable. You'd be on a sun lounger by a hotel pool having a drink and in five minutes he'd get distinctly uneasy and say we should be doing something more purposeful."[37]

"He had a vision that his life should be about helping people, doing meaningful, profound things. He thought he should be out there fighting for a cause," Chimes said.[38]

By this time, the tensions between Strummer and Jones had grown unbearable, and the band fired Jones. The band released a statement to the press announcing Jones's firing on September 1, 1983. "It is felt that Jones has drifted apart from the original idea of the Clash," wrote Strummer and Simonon in the statement. "In the future, [Jones's departure] will allow Joe and Paul to get on with the job the Clash set out to do from the beginning."[39]

Jones released his own statement, calling the band's account "untrue," adding that "there was no discussion with Strummer and Simonon prior to [my] being sacked."[40]

Later, Jones acknowledged that he was difficult near the end of his time in the Clash.

"The last couple of years in the Clash, I was a miserable

The Clash in 1983

git," Jones said. "We all knew that we were just doin' it for the money. We couldn't face each other. In rehearsals we'd all look at the floor. It was the worst."[41]

Jones's replacements were two guitarists—Vince White and Nick Sheppard—who made their live debut with the band on a series of shows on the West Coast in January 1984.

The new version of the group gave its first performance in Santa Barbara, California. Gone was the funk, reggae, and hip-hop experimentation. Instead, the Clash focused on straight-ahead punk.

"New guitarists Vince White and Nick Sheppard sounded as if they'd grown up solely on a diet of early Clash and Sex Pistols records," wrote Michael Goldberg in *Rolling Stone*. "Still, something was missing, and that something was the dynamic chemistry, a certain electricity, that once existed between Jones and Strummer."[42]

Strummer's political agenda was still one of anti-consumption. "Get up off your chair, turn off the TV, go outside and deal with real life. What I'm talking about in 1984 is the 'on' and 'off' switch on all appliances, and I would urge all Americans to put it in the 'off' position for a change. I turn off everything when I come here—TV, air conditioning," Strummer said.[43]

The new lineup went into the studio to record one album, 1985's *Cut the Crap*. Recorded in Munich, Germany, the mix was overseen by Bernard Rhodes and recording engineer

IN 1984, THERE WAS A NEW CLASH. FROM LEFT TO RIGHT: PAUL SIMONON, PETE HOWARD, JOE STRUMMER, VINCE WHITE, AND NICK SHEPPARD.

Simon Sullivan. Strummer was no longer in control. "I had a terrible time with Bernie in the end," Strummer said. "In a nutshell, in order to control me, he destroyed my self-confidence."[44]

When it was released in November 1985, *Cut the Crap* received withering criticism. *Rolling Stone*'s David Fricke called *Cut the Crap* "a cheat," and "the sound of the Clash just blowing smoke, thrashing in desperation under Strummer and bassist Paul Simonon's uncertain leadership."[45]

By the beginning of 1986, Strummer and Simonon split with the new members, and canceled British and American tour dates. The band had split from Rhodes and Vinyl and tried to make up with Jones, who wasn't interested. The Clash, finally, was finished.

Strummer realized pretty quickly that he had made a mistake by trying to continue the Clash. "Regret it? Oh, yeah. The Clash mark II was such a bummer. It was my then manager Bernie Rhodes' idea to get a new line-up and produce that album," Strummer said, adding that Rhodes didn't know what he was doing in the studio.[46]

Strummer felt remorse for firing Headon and Jones. "Whatever a group is, it was the chemical mixture of those four people that makes a group work. That's a lesson everyone should learn, 'Don't mess with it!' If it works just . . . do whatever you have to do to bring it forward, but don't mess with it. And, like, we learned that—*bitterly*."[47]

6

THE LAST GANG IN TOWN

As the final version of the Clash was sputtering to an end, Mick Jones was moving on. He formed a new band with Don Letts called Big Audio Dynamite (B.A.D. for short). B.A.D. released seven albums over the next decade.

In interviews surrounding the band's first album, Jones was clearly hurt by the split.

"I kept movin', and unfortunately they wanted to go backward," Jones said, adding that the split "should have happened a long time ago. But I happened to love the guys. They were like my family, so I never left. I always thought the best way was to work it out between ourselves and make it better."[1]

In the same *Rolling Stone* review that panned the Clash's *Cut the Crap, Rolling Stone* writer David Fricke celebrated Big Audio Dynamite's debut album. *"This is Big Audio Dynamite* hardly transcends the Clash's finest hours, but for Jones it is a new beginning. With *Cut the Crap,* one might well wonder if Joe Strummer's at the end of the road."[2]

The second B.A.D. album, *No. 10 Upping Street,* reunited Jones with Joe Strummer, who cowrote and produced more than half the album. But it wasn't a return to the power of the Clash's best work.

"The results, though, resemble B.A.D.'s initial offering more than anything the Clash ever did: the record is more challenging sonically than verbally," wrote *Washington Post* critic Mark Jenkins. "On songs like 'Beyond the Pale,' Strummer focuses Jones' meandering lyrics somewhat, but they still lack the immediacy of Clash communiques like 'Career Opportunities.' As on the last record, Jones sounds as though he's singing about things he's read about, not lived. The band's sound—a complex collage including Third World percussion, movie dialogue and dub effects—remains fascinating, but the actual songs are often unimpressive."[3]

In 2003, Jones teamed up with his old London SS partner Tony James to form a band called Carbon/Silicon. They released an album called *The Last Post* in 2007.

Topper Headon released a solo album titled *Waking Up* in 1986, but his heroin addiction was still out of control. He was

Mick Jones formed a new band—Big Audio Dynamite (B.A.D.).

selling his Clash gold record awards to pay for drugs, and in 1987, he was sent to prison for fifteen months for giving heroin to a friend who overdosed.

Paul Simonon formed a new band called Havana 3AM, which released a self-titled album in 1990. But, mostly, after the Clash ended, Simonon returned to his first love: painting. He launched a successful art career and abandoned music.

"There were a lot of people dying and being born around me, and I got on the path properly, which meant finding a good teacher and spending years in museums, drawing, drawing, drawing," Simonon said.[4]

Simonon returned to music in 2007, releasing an album with the Good, the Bad and the Queen, that also featured Damon Albarn from Blur and Gorillaz, Simon Tong from the Verve, and drummer Tony Allen from African legend Fela Kuti's band Africa 70.

For many years after the demise of the Clash, Strummer seemed lost. He acted in films like *Straight to Hell* and *Mystery Train* and contributed to soundtracks for the films *Sid and Nancy, Straight to Hell,* and *Walker.*

In 1989, Joe Strummer released an album called *Earthquake Weather* with a new band, called Latino Rockabilly War. Author Tony Fletcher wrote that that album "succeeded only in presenting Joe as a mediocre Bruce Springsteen."[5]

In 1991, he filled in with the Irish rock band the Pogues when that band's singer Shane MacGowan was ill. "According to those who saw his performances, they were among the finest of Strummer's life," wrote author Keith Topping.[6]

Mainly, though, Strummer was taking time to find himself. "I was burnt out by the intensity of five years with the Clash," he explained. "Then my parents died and my kids were born, which was a real one-two. When I was ready to come back, the difficulty was hooking up with people to work with—when you've been in a band as successful as The Clash there's a curtain around you. But I kept my energy. If I'd been playing for those 11 years I'd be a basket case by now—or a straitjacket case."[7]

Strummer finally formed a new band, called the Mescaleros, and resumed touring, releasing the albums *Rock Art and the X-Ray Style* in 1999 and *Global A Go-Go* in 2000.

As the twentieth century drew to a close, there was a flood of activity surrounding the Clash. The band's first live album, *From Here to Eternity,* was released, and the band members collaborated with Don Letts on a documentary called *Westway to the World*. But they still avoided the temptation to reunite.

"Reuniting would be artistic death," Strummer said in 1999. "It'd be like admitting defeat."[8]

"We all wanted to do the documentary, but we couldn't do it in the same room. It's still too heavy. We haven't been all together since Topper left," Strummer said.[9]

In 2003, the Clash were due to be inducted into the Rock

and Roll Hall of Fame. Many thought this would be the opportunity for the Clash reunion that so many hoped for. A mini-reunion of sorts took place in November 2002, when Joe and the Mescaleros played a benefit for the Fire Brigade Union in Acton, England.

Jones was in the audience. "When I heard the chords to 'Bankrobber,'" he said, "I just thought 'I've got to get up there.'"[10] He joined Strummer on stage and also played on "White Riot" and "London's Burning." It was the first time the two had performed on stage together for nineteen years.

That was the closest the Clash would come to a reunion. On December 23, 2002, Strummer died unexpectedly of a defective artery near his heart. Simonon's wife. Trisha, told *Rolling Stone,* "The coroner told us that it was a congenital problem. . . . It could have happened at any point in his life. He walked his dog, sat on his couch and died."[11]

Simonon said Strummer was trying to convince him to reunite for the Hall of Fame induction ceremony. "He tried to send me a fax that morning, the morning that he died," he said. "I didn't have a chance to reply unfortunately."[12]

Strummer's fax said: "Come on, Paul. Give it a try. You might even like it." But Simonon wasn't budging—he had no intention of playing the ceremony. "Joe was up for it, and so was Mick and Topper, but I wasn't," he said. "I was the one who always said no. In this instance, I really didn't believe it was the right moment. A big corporate event like that, two

In 2003, The Clash was inducted into the Rock and Roll Hall of Fame. From left to right: The Edge (U2 guitarist), Terry Chimes, Mick Jones, Paul Simonon, and Tom Morello (Rage Against the Machine guitarist).

grand a seat. Nah, that wasn't in the spirit of the Clash, was it?"[13]

In February, during the Grammy Awards, Bruce Springsteen, Dave Grohl, Elvis Costello, and Steven Van Zandt paid tribute to Strummer by playing "London Calling." A month later, the band was inducted into the Rock and Roll Hall of Fame. The surviving members did not play. U2 guitarist the Edge and Rage Against the Machine guitarist Tom Morello inducted the band.

"I loved this band," the Edge said. "To me, without doubt, they are next to the [Rolling] Stones as the greatest rock and roll band of all time. There is no doubt in my mind that [U2 song] 'Sunday Bloody Sunday' couldn't have been written if it wasn't for the Clash."[14]

Morello said that the band changed his life. The Clash "instilled in me the courage to pick up a guitar and the courage to try and make a difference with it," Morello said, adding: "I cannot imagine what my life would have been like without them."[15]

And, more than thirty years after the band first got together, there are many Clash fans who would agree with that sentiment.

TIMELINE

1976—Mick Jones, Paul Simonon, Joe Strummer, Terry Chimes, and Keith Levene form the Clash; Keith Levene and Terry Chimes both quit the Clash.

1977—The band signs with CBS Records; Terry Chimes rejoins the band and then leaves again; Nick "Topper" Headon joins the Clash.

1978—The Clash plays the Rock Against Racism rally in London; they fire manager Bernard Rhodes.

1979—The band tours the United States for the first time.

1981—They rehire Bernie Rhodes as manager; they play a series of dates at Bonds International Casino in New York.

1982—The band releases *Combat Rock*, which produces hit singles "Rock the Casbah" and "Should I Stay or Should I Go?"; just before a tour begins, Joe Strummer disappears to Paris; Topper Headon is fired because of his heroin addiction. Terry Chimes rejoins the band.

1983—Mick Jones is fired.

1984—Joe Strummer and Paul Simonon tour with a new version of the Clash featuring new members Nick Sheppard, Pete Howard, and Vince White.

1985—After releasing an album called *Cut the Crap* and embarking on an impromptu busking tour, the Clash disband.

2002—Joe Strummer dies.

2003—The Clash is inducted into the Rock and Roll Hall of Fame.

DISCOGRAPHY

CDs

1977 *The Clash (U.K.)*

1978 *Give 'Em Enough Rope*

1979 *The Clash (U.S.)*

1980 *London Calling*
Black Market Clash

1981 *Sandinista!*

1982 *Combat Rock*

1985 *Cut the Crap*

1988 *The Story of the Clash Volume I*

1991 *The Clash on Broadway*

1993 *Super Black Market Clash*

1996 *The Singles*

1999 *From Here to Eternity Live*

2003 *The Essential Clash*

2004 *London Calling: 25th Anniversary Edition*

2006 *Singles Vinyl Box Set*

2007 *The Singles*

2008 *Live at Shea Stadium*

DVDs

2002 *Westway to the World*

2003 *The Essential Clash*

2004 *Rude Boy (originally released 1980)*

2007 *The Future Is Unwritten*

2008 *Revolution Rock*

CONCERT TOURS

1976 First dates[1]
Anarchy in the UK Tour

1977 White Riot Tour
European '77 Tour
Out of Control Tour

1978 Sandy Pearlman dates
Rock Against Racism concert
Out on Parole Tour
Sort It Out Tour

1979 Pearl Harbor Tour
London Calling Tour
Take the Fifth Tour

1980 Sixteen Tons Tour of the U.K.
Sixteen Tons Tour of the U.S.A.
Sixteen Tons Tour of Europe

1981 Impossible Mission Tour
Bonds Residency N.Y.
Clash in Paris
Radio Clash Tour

1982 Far East Tour
Casbah Club U.S.A. and U.K. Tours
Combat Rock U.S.A. Tour

1983 US Festival Tour

1984 West Coast dates
Out of Control Tour

1985 Busking Tour and festival dates

GLOSSARY

anarchy—The absence of government; a situation where there is a lack of control.

bohemian—An artistic lifestyle that doesn't conform to that of conventional society.

busking—Playing music outdoors in a public place for spare change from passersby.

class—The division of society along economic and social lines.

communiqué—A message.

consumerism—Preoccupation with buying and consuming things.

dread—A person who wears a dreadlock hairstyle; a Rastafarian.

ethos—The philosophy of a particular culture.

genre—A classification or type. Punk rock, reggae, and new wave are genres of rock music.

gobbing—The practice of audience members spitting on bands to show appreciation, which was common in the 1970s punk-rock scene.

materialism—Valuing material goods and wealth over people.

Rastafarian—A member of a Jamaican religious group who believes that Ethiopian emperor Hailie Selassie I is a god.

reggae—A style of music that originated in Jamaica that features heavy accents on the second and fourth beats of a four-beat bar.

rockabilly—A style of rock and roll music from the 1950s that is influenced by country music.

squatting—The practice of taking over an abandoned property and living in it.

CHAPTER NOTES

Chapter 1: A Riot of My Own

1. "On This Day: 30 August 1976: Notting Hill Carnival Ends in Riot," *BBC News*, 2009, <http://news.bbc.co.uk/onthisday/hi/dates/stories/august/30/newsid_2511000/2511059.stm> (October 3, 2008).
2. *Westway to the World*, DVD, directed by Don Letts (1999; New York: Sony Music Entertainment, 2002).
3. Ibid.
4. *Seven Ages of Rock: Blank Generation*, documentary, directed by Alastair Lawrence (BBC/VH1 Classic, 2007).
5. Antonio D'Ambrosio, ed., "Let Fury Have the Hour," *Let Fury Have the Hour: The Punk Rock Politics of Joe Strummer* (New York: Nation Books, 2004), p. 4.
6. *Seven Ages of Rock: Blank Generation*.
7. Robert MacPherson, "Clash Frontman Joe Strummer Dead at 50," Agence France Presse, December 23, 2002.
8. Jon Pareles, "Honoring Rock's Past, Talking of Here and Now," *New York Times*, March 12, 2003.
9. "Why We Love the Clash," *NME*, May 19, 2007, p. 24.

Chapter 2: Who Are the Clash?

1. Caroline Coon, "The Clash: Down and Out and Proud," *Melody Maker*, November 13, 1976,

<http://www.rocksbackpages.com/article.html?ArticleID=10690> (April 4, 2007).

2. *Westway to the World,* DVD, directed by Don Letts (1999; New York: Sony Music Entertainment, 2002).

3. Ibid.

4. Bill Crandall, "Rock and Roll Hall of Fame: The Clash," *RollingStone.com,* February 28, 2003, <http://www.rollingstone.com/artists/theclash/articles/story/5937460/rock_and_roll_hall_of_fame_the_clash> (February 26, 2009).

5. *Westway to the World.*

6. Kristine McKenna, "A Man That Mattered," *Let Fury Have the Hour*, ed. Antonio D'Ambrosio (New York: Nation Books, 2004), p. 239.

7. Joe Strummer, Mick Jones, Paul Simonon, and Topper Headon, *The Clash* (New York: Grand Central Publishing, 2008), p. 23.

8. Paul Morley, "Clash USA '79," *NME*, October 13, 1979, <http://www.rocksbackpages.com/article.html?ArticleID=5600> (April 4, 2007).

9. Chris Salewicz, *Redemption Song: The Ballad of Joe Strummer* (New York: Farrar Straus and Giroux, 2007), p. 93.

10. Strummer, Jones, Simonon, and Headon, p. 16.

11. Marcus Gray, *The Clash: The Return of the Last Gang in Town* (London: Hal Leonard, 2004), p. 5.

12. Coon.

13. *Westway to the World.*

14. Gray, p. 16.

15. Pat Gilbert, *Passion Is a Fashion: The Real Story of the Clash* (Cambridge, Mass.: Da Capo Press, 2005), p. 39.

16. Gray, p. 19.
17. Ibid., p. 25.
18. Ibid., p. 16.
19. Sean O'Hagan, "The Buzzcocks Were Very Mondrian and We Were Very Pollock," *The Guardian* (Manchester), March 30, 2008, p. 14.
20. Ibid.
21. Ibid.
22. Ibid.
23. *Westway to the World.*
24. Gilbert, p. 152.
25. Strummer, Jones, Simonon, and Headon, p. 48.
26. Ibid., p. 337
27. Ibid., p. 377.
28. Ibid., p. 132.
29. Gray, p. 134.
30. Sean Coughlin, "Should I Stay or Should I Go Now?" *BBC News*, October 20, 2006, <http://news.bbc.co.uk/2/hi/uk_news/magazine/6060180.stm> (September 26, 2008).

Chapter 3: No Elvis, Beatles or the Rolling Stones

1. Jon Savage, *England's Dreaming* (New York: St. Martin's Griffin, 2001), p. 12.
2. Ibid., xiv–xv.
3. Caroline Coon, "The Summer of Hate," *The Independent* (London), August 6, 1995, p. 16.
4. Ibid.
5. *Westway to the World*, DVD, directed by Don Letts (1999; New York: Sony Music Entertainment, 2002).

6. Allan Jones, *Elgin Avenue Breakdown Revisited*, CD liner notes, Astralwerks.

7. *Joe Strummer: The Future Is Unwritten,* DVD, directed by Julien Temple (2007; Sony Legacy, 2008).

8. *Westway to the World.*

9. Mick Jones and Tony James interview, *Fresh Air*, National Public Radio, January 29, 2008.

10. Greg Shaw, "Sic Transit Gloria . . . : The Story of Punk Rock in the '60s," *Nuggets* box set liner notes, p. 22.

11. Kosmo Vinyl, *Clash on Broadway* CD box set liner notes, 2000, Epic/Legacy, p. 20.

12. Ibid.

13. Ibid.

14. Pat Gilbert, *Passion Is a Fashion: The Real Story of the Clash* (Cambridge, Mass.: Da Capo Press, 2005), p. 83.

15. *Clash on Broadway*, p. 20.

16. Stephen Thomas Erlewine, *All Music Guide*, 4th ed., ed. Vladimir Bogdanov, Chris Woodstra, and Stephen Erlewine (San Francisco, Calif.: Backbeat Books, 2001), p. 350.

17. Jonathan Dyson, "Out of Bondage," *The Independent* (London), March 27, 1999.

18. *Seven Ages of Rock: Blank Generation*, documentary, directed by Alastair Lawrence (BBC/VH1 Classic, 2007).

19. *Clash on Broadway*, p. 24.

20. *Westway to the World.*

21. Ibid.

22. Steve Walsh, "The Very Angry Clash," *Let Fury*

Have the Hour, ed. Antonio D'Ambrosio (New York: Nation Books, 2004), p. 24.

23. Joe Strummer, Mick Jones, Paul Simonon, and Topper Headon, *The Clash* (New York: Grand Central Publishing, 2008), p. 61.

24. *Seven Ages of Rock: Blank Generation.*

25. Chas de Whalley, "The Kursaal Flyers/Crazy Caravan/Clash: Roundhouse, London," *Sounds*, September 1976, <http://www.rocksbackpages.com/article.html?ArticleID=8031> (April 4, 2007).

26. *Westway to the World.*

27. Ibid.

28. Caroline Coon, "The Clash," *1988: The New Wave Punk Rock Explosion, 1977,* <http://www.rocksbackpages.com/article.html?ArticleID=5881> (April 4, 2007).

29. *Westway to the World.*

30. Pete Silverton, "The Clash: *The Clash*," *Sounds*, April 9, 1977.

31. Charley Walters, "Punk, Pretty Vacant Music," *Rolling Stone,* October 6, 1977, p. 103.

32. *Westway to the World.*

33. Sean Coughlin, "Should I Stay or Should I Go Now?" *BBC News*, October 20, 2006, <http://news.bbc.co.uk/2/hi/uk_news/magazine/6060180.stm> (September 26, 2008).

34. *Westway to the World.*

Chapter 4: London Calling

1. Eric Amfitheatrof "The Coloreds Must Go," *Time*, December 12, 1977, <http://www.time.com/time/

printout/0,8816,915825,00.html> (September 22, 2008).

2. Charlotte Cripps, Ben Naylor, Chris Mugan, and Colin Brown, "Rock Against Racism: Remembering That Gig That Started It All," *The Independent* (London), April 25, 2008, <http://www.independent. co.uk/arts-entertainment/music/features/rock-against-racism-remembering-that-gig-that-started-it-all-815054.html> (October 2, 2008).

3. Chris Salewicz, *Redemption Song: The Ballad of Joe Strummer* (New York: Farrar Straus and Giroux, 2007), p. 205.

4. Joe Strummer, Mick Jones, Paul Simonon, and Topper Headon, *The Clash* (New York: Grand Central Publishing, 2008), p. 172.

5. Ibid., p. 174.

6. Phil Sutcliffe, "The Clash: Rude Boy," *Sounds*, January 12, 1980, <http://www.rocksbackpages. com/article.html?ArticleID=3180> (April 4, 2007).

7. Ira Robbins, "The Clashmen Meet the Pearlman," *Trouser Press*, February 1979, <http://www. rocksbackpages.com/article.html?ArticleID= 1158> (April 4, 2007).

8. Ibid.

9. Greil Marcus, "The Clash: *Give 'Em Enough Rope*," *Rolling Stone*, January 25, 1979.

10. Barry Miles, "A Clash of Interests," *Sex, Drugs & Rock 'N' Roll*, ed. Jim Driver (New York: Carroll and Graf, 2001), p. 279.

11. Howie Klein: "The Clash: The Fillmore, San Francisco," *NY Rocker*, March 1979, <http://www.

rocksbackpages.com/article.html?ArticleID=10118> (April 4, 2007).

12. Don Snowden, "The Clash in L.A.: Just the Best," *LA Weekly,* February 23, 1979.

13. Harry Sumrall, "Diddley, Clash," *Washington Post,* February 16, 1979, p. D3.

14. *Westway to the World,* DVD, directed by Don Letts (1999; New York: Sony Music Entertainment, 2002).

15. *Making of 'London Calling': The Last Testament* documentary, directed by Don Letts (2004; New York: Sony Music Entertainment).

16. Ibid.

17. Chris Bohn, "The Clash: One Step Beyond," *Melody Maker,* December 29, 1979, <http://www.rocksbackpages.com/article.html?ArticleID=4504> (April 4 2007).

18. *The Last Testament.*

19. Bohn.

20. John Rockwell, "The Pop Life," *New York Times,* January 4, 1980.

21. Ibid.

22. Tom Carson, "The Clash: *London Calling,*" *Rolling Stone,* April 3, 1980.

23. Keith Topping, *The Complete Clash* (Richmond, Va.: Surrey, Reynolds & Hearn Ltd., 2003), p. 172.

24. Robert A. Hull, "The 'Radical' Best of Rock's New Wave," *Washington Post,* January 9, 1980, p. B4.

25. Salewicz, p. 277.

26. *Westway to the World.*

27. John Piccarella, "The Clash: Sandinista!," *Rolling Stone,* March 5, 1981, pp. 57–58.

28. Van Gosse, "The Clash: *Sandinista!*," *Village Voice*, January 14, 1981, <http://www.rocksbackpages.com/article.html?ArticleID=10398> (April 4, 2007).

29. *Westway to the World.*

30. *Joe Strummer: The Future Is Unwritten*, DVD, directed by Julien Temple (2007; Sony Legacy, 2008).

Chapter 5: Should I Stay or Should I Go?

1. Pat Gilbert, *Passion Is a Fashion: The Real Story of the Clash* (Cambridge, Mass.: Da Capo Press, 2005), p. 289.

2. "Opposite Sides of Brixton's Front Line," *BBC News*, April 7, 2006, <http://news.bbc.co.uk/2/hi/uk_news/4857456.stm> (September 22, 2008).

3. Joe Strummer, Mick Jones, Paul Simonon, and Topper Headon, *The Clash* (New York: Grand Central Publishing, 2008), pp. 302–304.

4. Paul Ramball, "Clash Credibility Rule," *NME*, October 10, 1981, <http://www.rocksbackpages.com/article.html?ArticleID=898> (April 4, 2007).

5. Ibid.

6. Ibid.

7. *Westway to the World*, DVD, directed by Don Letts (1999; New York: Sony Music Entertainment, 2002).

8. Bob Gruen and Chris Salewicz, *The Clash* (London: Omnibus Press, 2001), p. 240.

9. Gilbert, p. 294.

10. Geoff Edgers, "A Life of Revolution Rock," *Boston Globe*, December 25, 2002, p. E1.

11. Keith Topping, *The Complete Clash* (Richmond, Va.: Surrey, Reynolds & Hearn Ltd., 2003), p. 185.

12. Peter Hall, "The Clash to Release Single, LP," *Rolling Stone*, December 10, 1981, p. 77.

13. Peter Hall, "The Year of the Clash," *Rolling Stone*, August 19, 1982, p. 27

14. Ibid.

15. Ibid., p. 26.

16. Ibid.

17. Ibid.

18. David Fricke, "The Clash Bash Back," *Rolling Stone*, June 24, 1982, pp. 39, 42–43.

19. Ibid.

20. Charles Shaar Murray, "The Clash: Up The Hill Backwards," *NME*, May 29, 1982, <http://www.rocksbackpages.com/article.html?ArticleID=8054> (April 4, 2007).

21. Michael Goldberg, "The Clash: Revolution Rock," *Down Beat*, December 1982, <http://www.rocksbackpages.com/article.html?ArticleID=10420> (April 4, 2007).

22. Strummer, Jones, Simonon, and Headon, p. 346.

23. Kosmo Vinyl, *Clash on Broadway* CD box set liner notes, 2000, Epic/Legacy, p. 63.

24. Ibid.

25. Arthur Goldschmidt, Jr., *A Concise History of the Middle East* (Boulder, Colo.: Westview Press, 1988), p. 350.

26. Don Letts, *Culture Clash: Dread Meets Punk Rockers* (London: SAF Publishing, 2007), p. 150.

27. *Clash on Broadway*, p. 63.
28. "Lost and Found Dept: The Clash's Joe Strummer," *Rolling Stone*, June 24, 1982, p. 23.
29. Murray.
30. "Clash Drummer Bolts Band," *Rolling Stone*, July 8, 1982, p. 30.
31. *Westway to the World*.
32. Ibid.
33. Ibid.
34. *Joe Strummer: The Future Is Unwritten*, DVD, directed by Julien Temple (2007; Sony Legacy, 2008).
35. Alan Light, "Re:Masters: Mick Jones of the Clash," *MSN Music*, September 29, 2008, <http://music.msn.com/music/remasters/?icid=MUSIC1&GT1=MUSIC1> (October 3, 2008).
36. Interview, "Weekend All Things Considered," National Public Radio, July 14, 2007.
37. Sean Coughlin, "Should I Stay or Should I Go Now?" *BBC News*, October 20, 2006, <http://news.bbc.co.uk/2/hi/uk_news/magazine/6060180.stm> (September 26, 2008).
38. Ibid.
39. Christopher Connelly, "Mick Jones Fired From the Clash," *Rolling Stone*, October 13, 1983, p. 11.
40. Ibid.
41. Bill Flanagan, "Life After the Clash: Mick Jones Goes Bad," *Rolling Stone*, January 17, 1985, p. 36.
42. Michael Goldberg, "A Fired-up Joe Strummer Brings His New Clash to America," *Rolling Stone*, March 1, 1984, p. 43.
43. Bill Holdship, "The Clash: They Don't Want

to Spoil the Party So They'll Stay," *CREEM*, October 1984.

44. Topping, p. 188.
45. David Fricke, "The Clash: Cut the Crap / Big Audio Dynamite: This Is Big Audio Dynamite," *Rolling Stone*, January 16, 1986, p. 46.
46. Robert Sandall, "Wind of Change After the Clash," *The Times* (London), October 8, 1989.
47. *Westway to the World*.

Chapter 6: The Last Gang In Town

1. Bill Flanagan, "Life After the Clash: Mick Jones Goes Bad," *Rolling Stone*, January 17, 1985, p. 36.
2. David Fricke, "The Clash: Cut the Crap / Big Audio Dynamite: This Is Big Audio Dynamite," *Rolling Stone*, January 16, 1986, p. 46.
3. Mark Jenkins, "Post-Punk and Pro-Labor Party," *Washington Post*, December 5, 1986, p. N27.
4. Neil Spencer, "Review: Arts: A London Calling," *The Observer* (London), October 20, 2002, p. 6.
5. Tony Fletcher, *The Clash: The Complete Guide to Their Music* (London: Omnibus Press, 2005), p.107.
6. Keith Topping, *The Complete Clash* (Richmond, Va.: Surrey, Reynolds & Hearn Ltd., 2003), p. 213.
7. Neil Spencer, "When Punk Went Country," *The Observer* (London), July 1, 2001, p. 14.
8. Caroline Sullivan, "Reuniting the Clash Would be Artistic Death. It'd be Like Admitting Defeat," *The Guardian* (Manchester), September 24, 1999, p. 2.
9. Ibid.

10. Pat Gilbert, *Passion Is a Fashion: The Real Story of the Clash* (Cambridge, Mass.: Da Capo Press, 2005), p. 372.

11. Anthony DeCurtis, "Joe Strummer 1952–2002," *Rolling Stone*, January 23, 2003, p. 27.

12. Anthony Barnes, "Survivors of Punk Legend Rule Out Re-Forming," Press Association, March 1, 2003.

13. Sean O'Hagan, "The Buzzcocks Were Very Mondrian and We Were Very Pollock," *The Observer* (London), March 30, 2008, p. 14.

14. Wes Orshoski, "U.K. '70s Punk Prevails at 18th Hall of Fame," *Billboard*, March 22, 2003, p. 6.

15. Ibid.

• Tour History

1. Joe Strummer, Mick Jones, Paul Simonon, and Topper Headon, *The Clash* (New York: Grand Central Publishing, 2008); *Black Market Clash*, 2010, <http://homepage.mac.com/blackmarketclash> (June 1, 2010).

FURTHER READING

Bidini, Dave. *For Those About to Rock: A Road Map to Being in a Band.* Toronto, Canada: Tundra Books, 2004.

Gruen, Bob. *The Clash.* London: Vision On, 2004.

Handyside, Christopher. *Rock.* Chicago, Ill.: Heinemann Library, 2006.

Haskins, Jame. *One Love, One Heart: A History of Reggae.* New York: Jump at the Sun/Hyperion Books for Children, 2002.

Schaefer, A. R. *Forming a Band.* Mankato, Minn.: Capstone High-Interest Books, 2004.

The Clash. *The Clash: Strummer, Jones, Simonon, Headon.* New York: Grand Central Publishing, 2008.

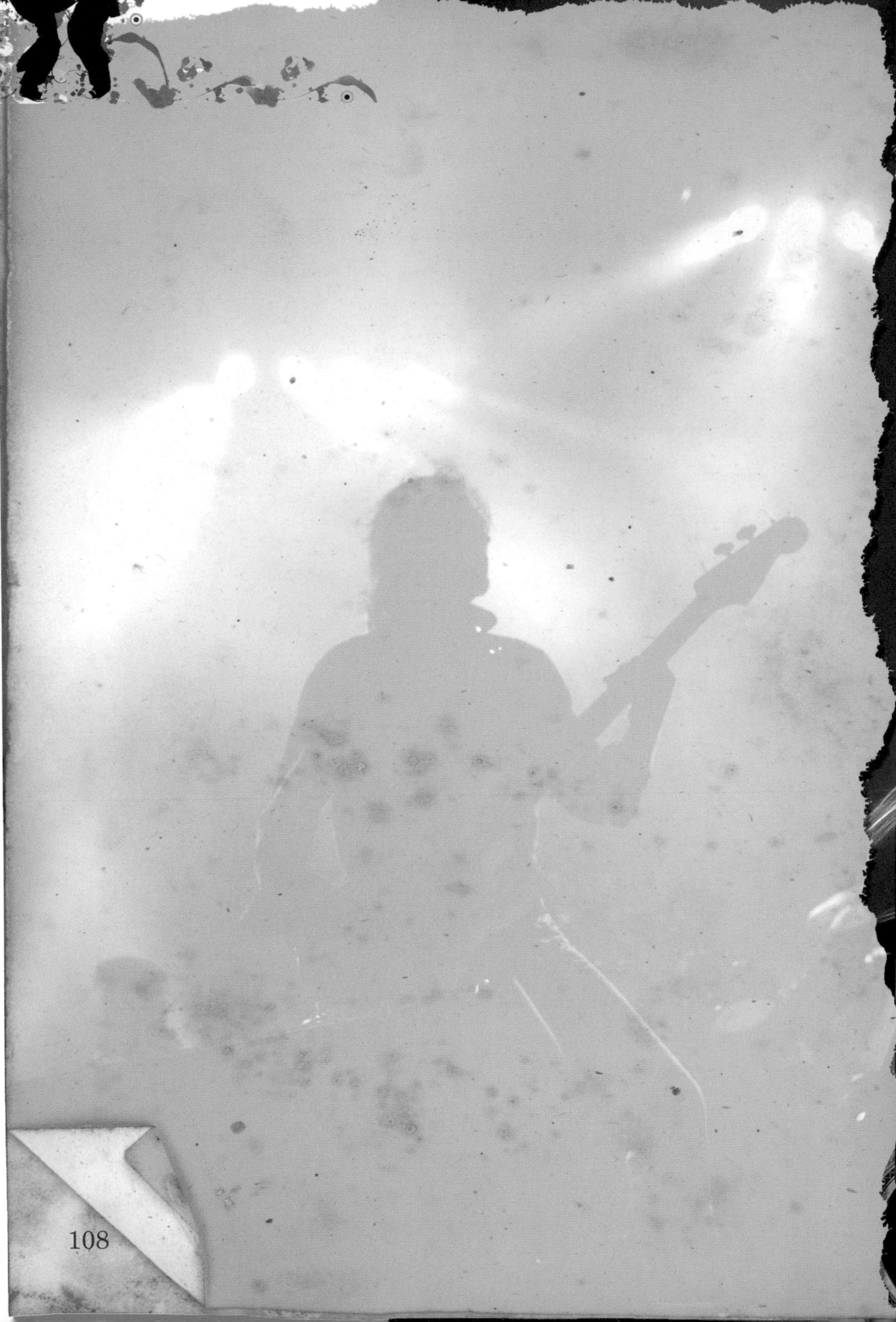

INTERNET ADDRESSES

The Clash, Sony Music Entertainment Site
<http://www.theclashonline.com/>

The Clash Official Site
<http://theclash.com/>

The Joe Strummer Foundation for New Music
<http://strummerville.com/>

INDEX